Collecting
Baseball
Memorabilia

Collecting Baseball Memorabilia

Thomas S. Owens

THE MILLBROOK PRESS
BROOKFIELD, CONNECTICUT

*To Mark Langill, Ray Medeiros,
and Diana Helmer, three friends who
preserve the fun, imagination, and
history of memorabilia.*

Photographs courtesy of The Topps Company: p. 8; The Upper Deck Company. UPPER DECK and the Upper Deck logo are trademarks of The Upper Deck Company. © 1995 The Upper Deck Company. All rights reserved. Used with permission.: p. 9; © 1994 Fleer Corporation: p. 11; Courtesy and © 1991 Cabin Fever Entertainment Inc., Greenwich, Ct. All rights reserved.: p. 14; Montreal Baseball Club Inc.: p. 16; Boston Red Sox: p. 16; The Minnesota Twins Baseball Club: p. 16; Los Angeles Dodgers: pp. 16, 44, 56; Mother's Cookies © 1996; author's collection: p. 21, 25, 60, 81; California Angels, registered trademark of Golden West Baseball Co.: pp. 27, 51; Vic Pallos: p. 29 (top: photo by John Pastier, bottom: photo by Ray Medeiros); Mississippi River Trading Company: p. 30; White Light Studio: pp. 33, 36, 55, 66 (bottom), 83 (top); General Mills, Inc.: p. 35 (Used with permission. Photo by White Light Studio); Tacoma News Tribune: p. 39; Reds Report: p. 40; Giants Public Relations: p. 45; Kansas City Royals: p. 47; Tacoma Rainiers Baseball Club: p. 59; San Diego Padres: p. 61; National Baseball Hall of Fame and Museum: pp. 66 (top), 69; Diana Star Helmer: p. 71 (both); Society for American Baseball Research: p. 74 (Illustration of Harvey Haddix courtesy Bill Perry Productions, Inc., and Gateway Stamp Co.); Baseball Chapel: p. 77; © Bruce Becker 1993, courtesy of Bill Goff, Inc., Kent, Ct.: p. 78; Baltimore Orioles: p. 83 (bottom); Donruss Trading Cards, Inc.: p. 91.

Library of Congress Cataloging-in-Publication Data
Owens, Thomas S.
Collecting baseball memorabilia / Thomas S. Owens.
p.   cm.
Summary: A guide for hobbyists and baseball enthusiasts who would like to expand their collections into other kinds of baseball memorabilia.
ISBN 1-56294-579-3 (lib. bdg.)
1. Baseball—Collectibles—United States—Juvenile literature.
[1. Baseball—Collectibles.] I. Title.
GV875.2.094   1996
796.357'02—dc20   95-19827   CIP   AC

Contents

Chapter One

◆

Beyond Baseball Cards

Bah! Humbug!

Ebenezer Scrooge, a character in Charles Dickens's famous story *A Christmas Carol,* was a miser who hated the holidays. The holidays, he said, were too commercialized, too stripped of meaning, an excuse for people to waste money and time. Happy holidays? Scrooge would scoff, "Bah! Humbug!"

Some baseball fans feel the same way about baseball cards. "Baseball cards? Bah! Humbug!"

But why wouldn't a fan like baseball cards?

After all, cards are colorful reference guides, listing the stats and career highlights of every major-league player for each major-league season. Cards might have cartoons, action photos, interesting facts about a player's past, artwork or holograms. Cards can be traded, displayed in scrapbooks, autographed by players, framed, even sold. Most of all, cards can help preserve the

memories of exciting games, maybe times shared at the ballpark or in front of the radio or TV with friends.

If a person likes baseball, what's not to like about cards?

They're too commercial, some fans say, meaning that the companies printing baseball cards—and the people who buy them—seem to care more about money than baseball.

The problem began in 1981, when the number of card companies tripled. To be different from one another, printers began making their sets brighter and bigger, adding special subsets with the promise of future profits for collectors. Hobbyists young and old began thinking about how valuable their sets might be in the future—instead of enjoying the hobby in the present.

So you think baseball cards come only in packs from hobby dealers? The only way to get one of these holograms produced by Upper Deck was to order a special meal at Denny's restaurant during the summer of 1994.

With more companies making cards, collectors began to have trouble keeping track of all the new cards. Rather than miss out on the "best" cards—those likely to rise in value—some collectors just gave up collecting.

Chase cards also created confusion. A hot trend of the 1990s, chase cards are randomly inserted cards that may appear once (or even less often) in an entire box of packs.

Some hobbyists burst open dozens of packs looking for just one type of insert card. (This is why companies call these hard-to-find creations "chase" cards.) These pack-poppers are inspired by price guides, which are magazines that list up-to-date selling prices of individual cards. Prices go up when people want an item, and new chase cards have high prices because everyone wants these cards—when they're new. When a new year brings another set of cards, those year-old inserts can quickly lose their appeal—and their supposed values.

Narrow-minded insert hunters don't care much for the "regular" sets. Those cards can be found in every pack!

High prices have prevented some fans from collecting. But price is just one factor; principle is another. Fans who feel that the game is the most important part of baseball are dismayed when a pack of baseball cards costs as much as a bleacher-seat ticket. Memories have meaning, these fans say. Isn't a memory of an actual game worth more than a mass-market memento?

In 1993, Fleer became the first manufacturer to issue a pack of $4 cards, the suggested retail price for a 10-card pack of a fancy set called Flair.

The baseball cards featured on this promotional sheet from Fleer may be easier to find than the sheet itself. Only card dealers and the media received these collectible promotional posters. Many probably were never displayed, and most probably were just thrown away.

The cards began at 40 cents apiece, even before dealers and price guides added to the price. When the minimum cost of a 300-card set reached more than $100, some hobbyists were stunned. After all, in 1983, just ten years earlier, a pack of 15 cards had cost 30 cents.

Even worse was the realization that many cards would not maintain their high investment prices. One year after Flair's debut, only a couple of cards still sold in the $10 to $15 range. The entire set averaged $75 to $100, which was a shock to those who had spent $150 or more putting a set together with packs. People who had been collecting baseball cards primarily as a means of investment began to feel they were on a road to nowhere.

WHY COLLECT ANYTHING ELSE?

Although investment-oriented collectors see baseball cards as a dead end, others see them as just the beginning of a journey. The cards teach collectors the ABCs of club and player histories. From these, it's easy to move on to more complicated baseball stories in yearbooks, hardcover books, photos from the past—whatever interests the collector. Some collectors look beyond baseball cards and see a hobby that is filled with baseball-related memorabilia.

What is memorabilia? Actually, it's anything you want it to be. Webster's *New Collegiate Dictionary* defines the word, coined in 1806, as "things that are remarkable and worthy of remembrance; things that stir recollection."

Suppose you see a jacket in the closet that you haven't worn in months. You empty the pockets and find a ticket stub, a tear-off tab that could be from anywhere. Then you find a pocket schedule of games of the minor-league team in the next town. That's where the ticket came from, the old-style high-school stadium the team uses. You remember now—the wooden seats, the cracked cement bathrooms, the close play that ended the game. What you found in your pocket "stirred recollections." Was your pocket full of trash or was it full of memorabilia?

If you've ever been to a professional ball game, think about what each fan brings home. Some people throw their ticket stubs away. Others hang on to them as mementos. The same goes for the pocket-size schedules that list the games.

Some spectators may save special cups from the concession stand (whether they had a drink or not!). Other fans seek autographs from the players.

Sure, most fans think of souvenirs as T-shirts, caps, pennants, yearbooks, and other goodies sold at or outside the stadium. Yet collectibles don't have to cost the contents of your piggy bank.

In fact, your bank may not oink at all at some low-cost souvenirs. For example, by buying a newspaper the day of the game and the day after, you'll have a detailed memory of the game, often complete with photos.

You don't have to choose to collect only baseball cards or only memorabilia. In fact, lots of collectors combine cards and memorabilia, and build unique displays to salute their favorite teams or players.

The emphasis of this book is on everyday mementos, not on one-of-a-kind, player-owned items, or products geared mainly to the hobby market. You

can find art prints, replica jerseys, autographed photo plaques, and other expensive collectibles at card shops or hobby shows, or on cable TV shopping shows. Dealers may sometimes note that only 10,000 or a similar "small" number of such limited editions are available.

High-priced items like these come and go in popularity, but there will always be ticket stubs, schedules, and other ordinary remnants from a baseball season available, whether you collect them or not. Actually, these easy-to-find items may disappear faster than the so-called "limited" collectibles, because fewer people think of saving ordinary stuff. That's why, if you don't throw away your "average" memorabilia, its value may someday allow you to sell or trade for more expensive stuff.

For hobbyists, the word "memento" refers to any item that creates a special memory. Even though a price guide may never value the autograph of the player you met, chances are you won't forget the adventure you had getting the signature. Did you have to wait for a signature in a crushing crowd of fans? Did the player ask you to toss your ball for him to sign, but he missed it and got bopped on the forehead? Did a player notice you and reach over the heads of the others because you were waiting so patiently?

Collecting inexpensive memorabilia is a hobby for collectors who love baseball, collectors who have heroes, collectors who root for the home team no matter how many games they lose or how low their cards drop in value.

Collecting memorabilia may confuse people like Scrooge who value everything about baseball in terms of money. You might have card-collecting friends who see your unique collection and say:

"That's not part of any set!"

"Those aren't in price guides. Will they ever be worth anything?"

"But those are so cheap to get, anyone could collect them!"

Non-card collectors take such remarks by other hobbyists as compliments. In fact, one of the joys of memorabilia comes from explaining what you have and why you collect it.

Collecting memorabilia allows you to set many of your own price limits. New baseball cards often have prices you can't control, because minimum suggested retail prices are set by the companies that print them. These companies also limit who can

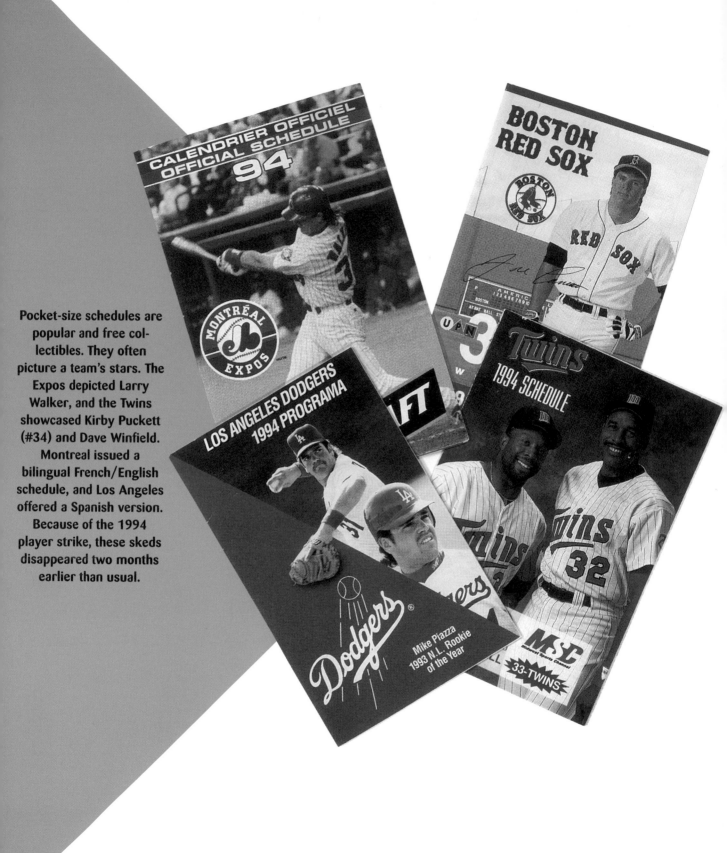

Pocket-size schedules are popular and free collectibles. They often picture a team's stars. The Expos depicted Larry Walker, and the Twins showcased Kirby Puckett (#34) and Dave Winfield. Montreal issued a bilingual French/English schedule, and Los Angeles offered a Spanish version. Because of the 1994 player strike, these skeds disappeared two months earlier than usual.

buy their cards by deciding who can sell them. Cards that can only be sold in card shops or retail outlets are harder for collectors to find.

A free team schedule, however, might be found at hundreds of retail locations, or even in your mailbox. And schedules are just the beginning. Schools and libraries also produce super collectibles: posters and bookmarks featuring famous athletes who are encouraging students to eat healthful foods, read, stay in school, and avoid drugs. Collectibles can be found on college campuses, in grocery stores and bookstores, often at low or even no cost. Bookstores may give away postcards picturing a new sports book. Grocery stores may throw away stand-up displays of athletes advertising food—unless a collector rescues those heroes.

A collection of baseball cards shows only the history of the players. A collection that includes more than baseball cards saves memories of players, games, and fans, especially you. You are as important to the game of baseball as the players. Where would baseball be without its fans? In a collection that goes beyond baseball cards, each item has a memory and a story. You can even build a story around your entire collection. Maybe your collection centers on all the ball games you've attended or that you've watched on television. The guidelines are up to you.

There are no sets you need to complete, or most valuable cards to acquire in the world of collecting memorabilia. People who collect only cards may open 75 packs to sort out and complete a set. Yet they probably don't remember which pack

IT'S UP TO YOU!

Frank Thomas's card was in, or what card number Ken Griffey, Jr., had.

With memorabilia, the old saying "The thrill is in the hunt" holds true. The effort of tracking down an autograph, a life-size stand-up of a famous player, or some other oddity is often a tale worth retelling. The story behind the collectible—a story that only you may know—can provide as much fun and value as the collectible itself.

When hunting for collectibles, don't overlook advertisements. This ad was given to stores selling Mother's Cookies to place in newspapers and magazines. A larger version of the poster was available as a store display.

Chapter Two

◆

Create Your Own Collectibles

*H*ow do you get beyond baseball cards? Where do you find memorabilia?

The search may be easier than you'd think. You might find what you're looking for right in your hometown, but first you need to know what you're looking for. To make your collection a one-of-a-kind creation, pick and choose from one or more of these hobby specialties:

AUTOGRAPHS

There's nothing more unique than an autograph. Try signing your name 10 times fast. You may spell it the same way, but every one of your signatures is bound to look a little different.

Autographs that you get in person almost always have a story attached. Maybe an All-Star picked you out of a crowd by saying, "Hey, Sunglasses. How are you doing?" and smiled while signing your program—writing so quickly that, if you hadn't been there, you wouldn't know who made that weird scribble on your book.

Sometimes, you might be the only one in a crowd of 100 fans who doesn't get an autograph. That can be an awful feeling, and you might even decide never to ask for an autograph again. Instead, consider asking in a different way. Without pushing or yelling, it is possible to get a player's exclusive attention.

Let the postal service do the work! Write to the player in care of the team and ask for an autograph. Include the card you want signed and be sure to enclose a self-addressed, stamped envelope (S.A.S.E.) so the team member can answer quickly and easily. Even if players get paid zillions of dollars, they don't have time to run to the post office to buy stamps, and tear and lick and stick them. (If you write for a lot of autographs, you'll see that the cost of postage stamps can add up quickly!) But if you take care of this expense with your S.A.S.E., the player may be able to return the favor by sending you a photo.

Of course, the best way to be sure to get a photo is to ask for one. Likewise, if you'd like a player to include your name in the autograph, be sure to ask politely. Beginning in the 1980s, dozens of players who were asked for in-person autographs insisted on personalizing each signature: "To (Somebody's Name)." Surprisingly, these players admitted that addressing an autograph to an individual fan was for their own protection. If "To Tony" appeared on each signed collectible, selling the items (except to someone else named Tony) would be nearly impossible.

FAMILY
FUN
CENTER
STEVE MURA

Why should players care if someone sells their autographs?

An autograph is a gift from the player, thanking a fan for support. Gifts are meant to be treasured, not sold to the highest bidder.

Therefore, think about the player's feelings when writing with a request. Write a personal letter of one page or less. Send only one item to be signed. Busy superstars who still answer autograph requests often sign just one card sent by fans and return the rest blank.

In your letter, tell the player how you learned about him. Did you see the player in person during his rookie season, or through radio or TV broadcasts? Maybe you discovered the player while he was playing in the minor leagues—or on a college team! List the year. It won't hurt to mention if you saw or heard about his game-winning hit or record-setting pitching performance, either. If you have 25 different cards of that player or other items about him in your collection of memorabilia, mention that, too.

Tell what item you're sending, whether it's a card, a drawing you made yourself, or any other memorabilia that would be easy to mail. If you also want a photo, ask. Even a famous player may think you don't want a photo if you didn't ask for one. If you do ask for a photo, you probably won't know what size the photo might be. Today, most team-produced photos are 3 1/2 by 5 1/2 inches (the size of postcards), designed to fit neatly into regular envelopes. Back in the 1970s the New York Mets furnished players with 4- by 5-inch glossy photographs to use for autographing. Fans were often thrilled to find a surprise bonus with the replies to their letters, but would cringe at how the once-mint photo was creased and folded to fit into a small envelope. If you send an envelope that will hold a 5- by 7-inch photo, or even an 8 by 10, remember to paste on extra stamps and to provide a piece of cardboard that will protect the photo on its postal trip to your home.

Because superstars may get more than 100,000 letters per year, your letter and item to be signed could get separated. That's why you should include your address in the letter, too, and remind the player that you did send an S.A.S.E.—even if it got lost in his locker!

Here's a sample letter:

Dear Mr. <u>(insert name)</u>:

I'm a fan of yours and the <u>(insert name)</u> team, win or lose. I first started following your career in <u>(insert year)</u>, when <u>(briefly describe a memorable accomplishment the player or team achieved during the year mentioned)</u>.

I collect autographs and would be grateful if you would sign the enclosed <u>(insert name of item)</u>. Please sign it "To <u>(insert your name)</u>," if possible. If you could provide a picture of yourself, I'd be very happy.

Thank you for your time. I've enclosed a self-addressed, stamped envelope for your reply. Good luck to you and your teammates!

Sincerely,

<u>(sign here)</u>
<u>(insert your name, and address)</u>

Some busy, popular players wait until the off-season winter months to answer all mail. But some players don't answer at all. Why? Sometimes, letters just get lost. Sometimes, players fear that fans want autographs just to sell them. Finally, the most popular players are likely to get more mail and are just too busy to answer it all. A rookie, part-time player probably receives fewer letters, so he'll have more time and energy to send a reply. The same holds true for former players who work as radio and TV announcers. Don't forget them in your autograph hunt.

Minor-league teams are sometimes overlooked as resources for by-mail autographs. Some have top draft picks from colleges and high schools, major leaguers recovering from injuries, and retired big leaguers who coach. But how can a signature hound sniff out where these players are?

Since the 1970s, collectors have relied on one book to help them contact players at their homes. Every two years, *The Baseball Address List* (published by Sports Americana) is compiled by collecting pioneer Jack Smalling. Through endless detective work, Smalling tracks down the home addresses of nearly all active and former big-league players, umpires, and coaches. With this reference book, it's easy to write to almost any living person in the field of baseball.

If you don't have a collectible card to send to a player, try sending a 3- by 5-inch index card. While a plain white card might look boring to some collectors, it gives a player space to write a personal greeting if he chooses.

It's possible to dress up index cards, too. For example, you could neatly paste on the card tiny mug-shot photos of the player you cut from the newspaper. Or you could draw your own portrait of the player. How about adding a team logo or sticker? Because it is different or unique, your request might rocket to the top of the fan-mail pile. Remember, the only rules about items worth autographing are the rules that you yourself make up.

Once you get your autographs, keep in mind that the signatures on the fronts of baseball cards,

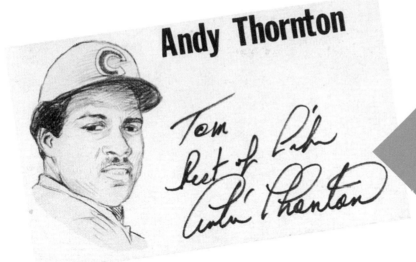

Andy Thornton

Tom
Best of Luck
Andre Thornton

The "3 by 5,"
the hobbyist's term
for an autographed
index card, can be made more
interesting with a drawing, sticker,
lettering, or photo. In the 1970s an
enterprising autograph collector
and dealer created special cards
like this one for hobbyists
to send to their
favorite players.

either in ballpoint or permanent ink (from "Sharpies" or other special pens) can smudge. Ink can also fade from constant exposure to light. So keep your souvenirs inside their original envelopes (the postmark is proof of the response and part of the collection), or in plastic sheets designed to hold cards.

Autographed pictures and cards need to breathe inside their plastic sheets. Humidity can trap moisture, which isn't healthy for paper. Remove the cards for a couple of hours every six months or so to check for moisture, and to make sure that the chemicals inside the sheets are not absorbing the ink off a signed photo. Although the memory of getting an autograph may last forever, the actual signature might not be as lucky without some tender, loving care.

Imagine sending a surprise selection of one dozen baseball cards to a collector you've never met. She sends you back the same number of cards. Neither one of you has checked a price guide beforehand.

SCHEDULES

This doesn't happen with card collectors, but that's the life of a "skedder" or "skedhead," two popular nicknames for collectors of team schedules, or "skeds." This kind of blind trading happens regularly. Some collectors even send back more schedules than they receive, happy that they can help another hobbyist.

No price-guide magazines exist for schedules. It's a simpler hobby than card collecting, one without the usual complete sets that card collectors know. Sked collectors have different goals. Some want one schedule each year from every big-league team. Other more active collectors will want all the schedules from all the teams, including every club represented in the minor leagues.

Some sked fans may focus on only one team, and look for advertising variations. A team like the Phillies may seem to have only one schedule, but different versions with ads from different sponsors may create new possibilities for collectors. Some adult collectors want only those pocket skeds from their favorite soda or beer company.

Skeds can appear on posters, magnets, bottles, cups, or other objects. But the favorites in hobby circles are still the paper, pocket-size team schedules. These often contain pictures of stars from the team or a photo of the mascot or stadium. A schedule may include a slogan or motto the team will use all season. For example, the 1991 St. Louis Cardinals sked read: "Where Legends Come to Play." Some teams will salute a special anniversary or last year's championship on their skeds.

Inside, a diagram of the team's stadium may be included, showing which seats you could buy

1990 ANGELS
BASEBALL SCHEDULE
TICKETS AVAILABLE NOW

Not all schedules
are pocket size. In 1990
the California Angels
designed this 4- by 9-inch
schedule to be displayed
with travel brochures and
other tourism materials.

at what prices. Some skeds have a list of days in which everyone attending gets a free souvenir or collectible to bring home.

A few collectors may laugh at skedding, because these team schedules are free by mail, or can be picked up at no cost in a team's region in sporting-goods stores, grocery stores, or anywhere tickets are sold.

Most schedules, however, get shoved into purses or wallets and are crumpled and torn by the season's end. Most fans throw them away, and wait for next year's.

Meanwhile, you keep yours, and in good condition, too. While the price-guide magazines may not show it, your surviving sked may be more rare than any baseball card made that year.

STADIUM POSTCARDS

Arranging a trip to a big-league stadium may be difficult and costly, but getting a look at your favorite ballpark can be cheap and easy.

For more than a century, picture postcards have been a way for visitors to keep and to share unique views of special scenery. Even collectors who have made many visits to a stadium can be amazed at the new perspectives that postcards offer.

One noted angle is the overhead shot: how the stadium looks from the sky. At a flea market or a sports-collectibles show, dealers might ask prices averaging $10 to $25 for postcards of famous torn-down stadiums, such as Ebbets Field in Brooklyn or the Polo Grounds in New York. Believe it or not, some hobbyists have only paid from 25 cents to $2 for postcards of these same ballparks.

If you know your stuff, everything's cheaper. Instead of diving into a dealer's pile of expensive "ballpark" postcards, check the dealer's stack of cards from the city or state where favorite teams play. Look for those hidden pictures. Advanced collectors have found famed landmarks peeking out of aerial longshots on postcards from the 1940s and 1950s captioned "New York Skyline" or something similar. Undiscovered treasures will be the cheapest.

Be warned, though, that postcard collectors can fall into the same "mint only" trap that snares their sport-card-chasing counterparts. Watch for the flea-

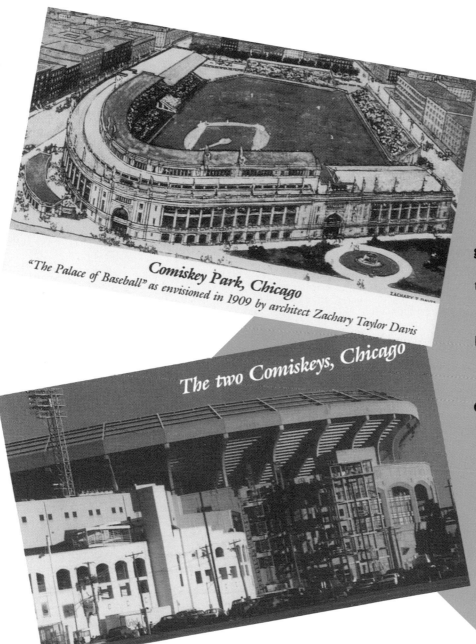

Comiskey Park, Chicago
"The Palace of Baseball" as envisioned in 1909 by architect Zachary Taylor Davis

The two Comiskeys, Chicago

Postcards are a great way to have a look at a stadium that is far away—or that no longer exists. In this set, producer Vic Pallos presents the first drawing of Chicago's original Comiskey Park. The second card shows the new and old Comiskey Parks, side by side.

Postcards are
an inexpensive collectible,
and sometimes they contain
hidden treasures. Both of these cards
show a baseball game in progress,
but the aerial night shot
also shows the 1987
World Series in St.
Louis, Missouri.

market dealers or hobby-shop owners who insist that their vintage postcards are high-priced because they've never been handled, written on, or mailed, and are in "mint" condition.

History-loving hobbyists know the used postcard in less than mint condition is more affordable, more informative, and more fun. Granted, when a card travels through the mail, there will probably be an expected crease or other sign of wear. Yet a postcard that was actually sent has many extras never enjoyed by a mint duplicate. For instance, imagine spotting a message written to a friend of 50 years ago, telling of a home run smashed by a future Hall of Famer or of the roaring crowd at a World Series game.

Thanks to the postmark, the proof of the witnessed moment in history is on the postcard. For example, if you find a Forbes Field postcard postmarked June 28, 1970, from Pittsburgh, you have a souvenir with official government proof from the last game the Pirates played in their old home stadium. Look for postcard cancellations, then check a baseball-history book to see how the team at the ballpark was doing when the card was mailed. If you attend a memorable game in the future, such as a World Series or an All-Star contest, mail yourself a postcard! Some post offices even offer specially designed postage cancellations right at the ballpark for extra-special events.

Don't worry if you can't afford, or even find, antique postcards of stadiums from 50 to 75 years ago. Beginning in the 1970s, some collectors realized that hard-to-find, older examples of ballpark postcards were too expensive for beginning collectors. To let more people enjoy the hobby, these collectors printed their own retrospective postcards. By using photos from the past and writing new captions for the backs of their self-published postcards, these hobbyists provided low-cost alternatives for other hobbyists.

Every year, look for new postcards of current baseball parks. Both the inside and outside of a stadium can change yearly, and postcards can record the growth and development of a ballpark. Look closely at interior pictures. Some shots may feature pregame festivities during All-Star or World Series games, which make them more collectible.

Also, some postcards may have the same picture, but different captions, such as "Home of the 1993 World Champions" or "Host of the 1994 All-Star Game." Don't expect these dated cards to stay on store racks for more than one year.

No matter how old or new, keep postcards stacked tightly in a box so they don't bounce around and get damaged. The thin postcard paper can become fragile over the years, so don't bundle cards together with rubber bands. Even if the band doesn't cut notches into the postcard's sides, the rubber can discolor some items.

New postcards should not be hard to find if you do any traveling near baseball towns. Once you find a collectible postcard, consider buying an extra one to mail back home to yourself as a lasting document of your trip to the ballpark.

FOOD FINDS   No matter where you live, a nearby grocery store or restaurant just might have a surprising collectible for you.

Breakfast cereals, for example, may be a great way to start your day, and your collection. In the 1990s, Kellogg's signed a deal that made their cereals Major League Baseball's "official" cereals. This gave the company the right to print photos of players and team logos on box fronts and backs. In 1993, Kellogg's Corn Flakes boxes sported a picture of legendary pitcher Nolan Ryan. Ken Griffey, Jr., was seen on Sugar Frosted Flakes. A year before, Tony the Tiger was seen on a set of boxes, wearing the uniforms of many different teams. Hobbyists had to hustle for these regionally distributed boxes. Tony as a San Diego Padre, for example, was available mainly in Southern California.

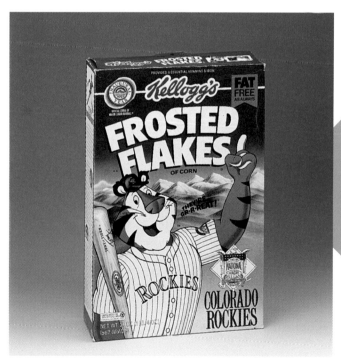

Kellogg's made a deal in 1993 that made it the official cereal company of Major League Baseball. This meant that no other companies could put team logos on breakfast-cereal boxes. This regional issue was supposed to be sold only in the area of Denver, Colorado; the author found it on the shelf of a grocery store in central Iowa.

In 1991, six Corn Flakes box backs had action shots of six Hall of Famers: Hank Aaron, Ernie Banks, Yogi Berra, Lou Brock, Steve Carlton, and Bob Gibson. Kellogg's provided instructions for cutting out the figures and making three-dimensional stand-ups. Smart collectors didn't cut up the boxes.

Keeping a collectible in its original condition helps maintain its financial worth, but, most important, preserves its history. What size of cereal box offered the cutouts? What year were they issued? The answers are on the original box.

Full, unopened cereal boxes can fill up a collector's room quickly. Keeping boxes full of food can cause other problems, too. Bugs and rodents may become your unwelcome visitors, searching for the edible contents of your collectibles. Some boxes may leak cereal if the inner bag breaks.

A safe alternative is to remove the bag of cereal, then gently open both the top and bottom box flaps. Now you can flatten the box carefully along its folds. This same treatment is recommended for other consumer packaging that might offer sports collectibles.

Some of the products that have featured cards, posters, and photos over the years include gelatin, pizza, snack-size cakes, bread, crackers, chips, and dog biscuits. That's right, dog biscuits offered cards in the early 1990s depicting players at home with their pets. So when you search the grocery for sports cards, leave no bone unturned.

The soda-pop aisle of the supermarket may yield treasures, too. Though many brands feature

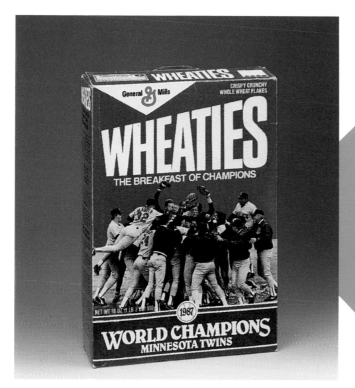

The back of this box of Wheaties, issued only in the Midwest in 1988, features a photo of the entire Minnesota Twins team. Flat storage is the safest, easiest way to keep cereal boxes, but be sure to remove all the food contents first!

commemorative art, Coca-Cola has out-issued other rivals with the most baseball-related cans and bottles over the years.

Cans can be challenging to collect. The safest way to keep a can is to ask an adult to punch two holes in the bottom with a can opener, then drain the pop slowly. Rinse the can with water, let it dry, then stand it up again. Your collectible will look like it's never been opened! But if a can is actually left unopened for years, it may rust, leak, or even explode because of temperature changes. Unopened bottles, however, pose no storage problems—although a glass bottle of 15-year-old pop probably won't taste very good.

When deciding which food collectibles to hunt, look at the player photos closely. Unlike Kellogg's, some companies save time and the fees charged by Major League Baseball (MLB) by airbrushing pictures to remove team names or logos from the players' uniforms. These symbols are owned by MLB, which wants to be paid when a company is going to use them to make money.

Not all food premiums are included on the package. Some companies want you to buy more than one package, maybe even different products, and mail both the box tops and money in order to receive your prize. You need to decide if the col-

Some food companies offer collectible premiums—but you may have to mail in some proof of purchase and sometimes money, too. This 1993 "collector package" of Kellogg's Corn Flakes, offering hobbyists a souvenir team helmet, features Nolan Ryan, who was then in his last season as an active player.

lectible offered is worth the price—especially if you really don't like the food!

Food-related memorabilia offer hobbyists a bonus. How often do you get a reward for eating and drinking? Telling the story of how you acquired a unique card from a pizza company is another fun dividend.

Food companies aren't the only ones offering collectible premiums. Grocery stores, for example, might offer a different poster each week with a minimum purchase. Or a fast-food chain may picture that area's players on cups or placemats. There are also collecting opportunities even when food isn't involved. Get adults you know into the act: Gas stations, banks, and corporations often use free bonuses to convert fans and collectors into customers.

SCRAPBOOKS

Even though a scrapbook starts out as a bunch of blank pages to paste scraps of paper on, your organization and creativity can turn a scrapbook into a time machine, a way for others to travel with you into baseball's past.

Focus on the "book," not the "scrap." Just like a book publisher, you decide what stays in the final copy and what is left out. In your scrapbook, readers get to see your perspective on certain players, teams, or entire seasons. Think of your scrapbook as a time capsule. What will be the highlights of this baseball season? What moments would you want to remember years from now?

Plan carefully before beginning a scrapbook. Use your imagination when deciding which items will be displayed there: newspaper or magazine clippings, photos, or other flat collectibles small enough to fit or fold into your scrapbook pages. You may want to leave room to write on the page, explaining why a pictured player or specific game was special to you.

Don't paste any paper goods such as cards, autographs, or photos on a page if you're concerned about their future values. Although tape may seem quicker and neater than rubber cement, tape will not only lose much of its stickiness over the years, but will also discolor many paper goods. Rubber cement often adheres better and stains less. For anything that has potential value, use adhesive photo corners, which are available in photo or stationery stores. These corners are like tiny pockets,which stick to the scrapbook page and allow you to slip the card or photo in and out without rips or damage from glue spots.

If you don't live near your favorite team, it may be difficult to find news clippings for your scrapbook. After all, newspapers in Texas will give more ink to the Rangers and Astros than to the Cincinnati Reds. But don't give up. Many cities across the country sell daily newspapers from major American cities such as New York or Chicago. If your search at the local newsstand reveals nothing, check out your public library. Libraries often receive major metropolitan papers on a weekly, or even daily, basis and may be willing to give them to you when they're no longer needed.

Ask a librarian how long those papers are kept on file. The librarian may remove and recycle them after a week or a month and keep only microfilmed versions. If this is the case, explain why you want the papers and ask if you could pick them up when they're ready to be discarded.

THE NEWS TRIBUNE

SOUNDLIFE

HABITAT

You can include more than just the daily newspaper accounts of games in your scrapbook. In 1992, Washington state's News Tribune featured the work of baseball artist Anthony Douglas. This article would fit in collections of collectibles about the Tacoma Tigers; their parent team, the Oakland Athletics; the California Angels (catcher's uniform); player-turned-coach Bob Boone; or Boone's son Bret, who is also a big leaguer.

◀ **A BERRY GOOD YEAR**
A little late-season labor will bear fruit next year;
George Pinyuh, 2

◀ **ADVICE TO CHEW ON**
Cancer studies warn heedless teenagers that smokeless tobacco use can snuff out lives; **14**

DRAWING INTO THE LEAD

Tacoma Tigers' Baseball Card Show will feature a sports artist with winning style; **3**

SATURDAY, AUGUST 8, 1992 • SECTION D

◀ **ADIOS OLYMPICS**
NBC set for finale of Barcelona Games;
Jon Burlingame, 20

◀ **INSIDE**

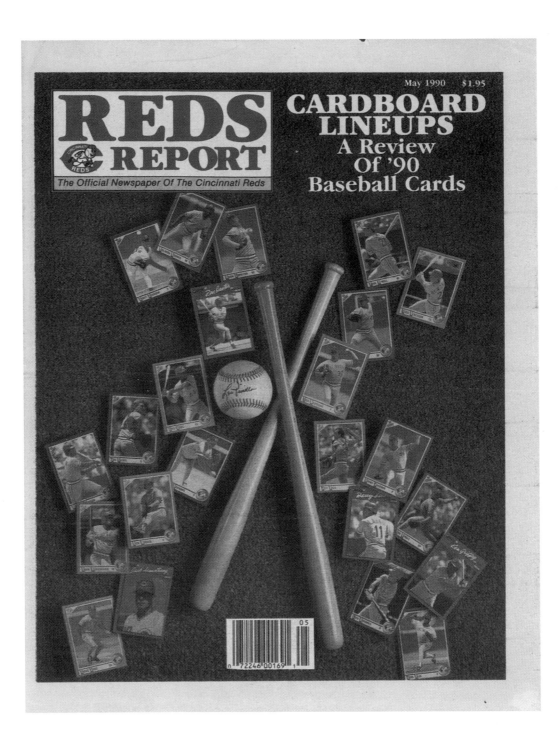

May 1990 $1.95

REDS REPORT
The Official Newspaper Of The Cincinnati Reds

CARDBOARD LINEUPS
A Review Of '90 Baseball Cards

You can also photocopy the article from the library's copy of the newspaper. You can copy just the photo, just the headline, the story and headline without the photo, or the entire article.

Computer users know that more material for scrapbooks may be available on-line each year and can simply be downloaded and reprinted. The Seattle Mariners, following the 1994 season, became the first major-league baseball team to go on-line. Press releases, schedules, rosters, and mail-order souvenir lists were a few of their first offerings.

As you assemble your scrapbook, remember that it will be more than the story of a season or a team. Your scrapbook will tell your family and friends and other future readers about yourself and about the world you lived in when the book was made. For example, scrapbooks made by collectors of the 1950s, perhaps your parents or grandparents, displayed magazine color photos in places of honor because most media at that time (even television) were produced in black and white.

The challenges of your world are part of your history. Record it all. Your distance from your favorite out-of-state team, or your lack of money to collect all the memorabilia you desire, or your old computer's inability to reproduce baseball finds nicely may be tough opponents, but they can't defeat a patient and imaginative collector.

Use your imagination to add to this chapter's list of unusual, low-cost collectibles.

Team-specific publications, some produced by the teams themselves, are good sources of material for scrapbook makers. Newspapers like the Reds Report combine articles about the team's season with articles about collectibles.

Chapter Three

◆

Team Treasures

Young sports and baseball fans often think that they can never become collectors. Usually, they list three barriers: age, address, and income.

Can a dedicated hobbyist overcome one, or all, of these shortcomings? Absolutely! This chapter and the next include some game plans for combating hobby hang-ups.

Younger collectors sometimes envy adults who can buy game-worn uniforms, used bats, even the seats from torn-down stadiums. Many such exclusive collectibles have been available for purchase since the 1980s, when major-league teams realized that their trash could be some fan's treasure. Equipment that was once discarded began to be sold in official team stores and in stadium gift shops.

Younger, beginning memorabilia fans often believed that such team-sponsored treasures could not be acquired by kids unless they were bat girls or had major-league dads. The truth is, when it comes to acquiring classy, limited-edition collectibles for little or no cost at all, young fans have opportunities that adults can only dream of. Sure, adults can buy items that kids can't afford. But only kids can go to specially advertised major-league games and receive souvenirs "free to all fans ages 12 and under."

You can bet there are adult collectors who envy the kids who get caps, coolers, seat cushions, or even toy mascots just for attending a game. Some grown-ups actually barter with youngsters, offering to buy tickets to the game if the kid will turn over the prize given for attending. Some adults even offer to buy or swap for a child's collectible right in the stadium aisles.

Teams once believed that practical premiums such as T-shirts, caps, or bats would be the most appealing goodies to be passed out at games. Since then, memorabilia mania has inspired many clubs to produce card sets, photos, pennants, posters, pins, and publications.

Premiums are often out in full force during the last weeks of the season, when nearly all teams have "fan appreciation" promotions. Many teams seem to clean out their merchandise closets, trying to get rid of kid premiums from two weeks ago, adult premiums from two months ago. Normally, if you don't get the item during the one game in which it is issued for free, it is no longer available anywhere for any price. Collectors consider these bonus giveaways the best parts of fan appreciation promotions, even though publicity stunts—such as giving away season tickets, cars, and trips—often overshadow the giving away of "leftovers."

PROMOTIONS AND PREMIUMS

For their weekend home opener, the Dodgers created this calendar for those fans attending the game. Each month's "pinup" is a photo of an actual baseball card.

October

Sunday	Monday	Tuesday	Wednesday	Thursday	Friday	Saturday
November S M T W T F S 1 2 3 4 5 6 7 8 9 10 11 12 13 14 15 16 17 18 19 20 21 22 23 24 25 26 27 28 29 30						1 San Francisco 7:05 p.m. GIANTS KABC •KWKW
2 San Francisco 1:05 p.m. Fan Appreciation Day GIANTS KABC • KWKW	3	4	5	6	7	8
9	10 Columbus Day (Observed)	11	12	13	14	15
16	17	18	19	20	21	22
23	24 United Nations Day	25	26	27	28	29
30	31 Halloween	Order your Dodger tickets using VISA or MasterCard by calling: (213) 224-1-HIT		GREAT WESTERN BANK GW A Federal Savings Bank KTLA 5 LOS ANGELES 790 KABC TALKRADIO KWKW 1330AM La Mexicana		

Promotional games are great for collectors who live near a major-league ballpark or stadium. Hobbyists farther away may be able to plan trips or vacations with premium nights in mind. But for many collectors, young and old, the nearest big-league city is hundreds of miles away, and years may pass without a trip to the ballpark. It's still possible to have your favorite team come to you. With some persuasive letter-writing and a few postage stamps (or adult-approved on-line transmission), fans of any age in any location can have access to an entire major-league organization.

Welcome to Candlestick Park

Important Information for Giants Fans

The San Francisco Giants offered a brochure to fans at the stadium—and to anyone considering buying a ticket. The brochure unfolds into a mini-poster outlining the team's history.

COLLECTING BY MAIL

Do you think that kids can't compete with adults in collecting baseball memorabilia? On paper or computer screens, kids can. Players and teams don't ask the age of fans who write to them. Mention that you have a collection of thousands of team cards, that you buy the products of the companies who sponsor a team's radio and television broadcasts, or even that your parents bring you to several games each year.

Teams will not send free fan-night premiums through the mail. But most teams will send schedules, stickers, rosters, and player photos for almost no cost at all. Many of these items are not available in gift shops or at fan-night giveaways, which makes them true collectibles. During after-season sales, some teams send merchandise catalogs or souvenir lists, which allow you to purchase overstocked premiums or items from past years.

Current major-league team addresses are printed often in most hobby magazines and appear yearly in almanacs and other reference books available at school or public libraries. It's important to get the newest addresses possible. Teams move to different stadiums or new towns. Just because the Baltimore Orioles are in Baltimore and the mail carriers know about the team, this doesn't mean your letter will be delivered if you send it to the team's old ballpark, Memorial Stadium.

A brief, specific request on a postcard can save you time and money. *Baseball America* publishes a yearly directory in pocket-size paperback form, listing the addresses of all front-office team members: the people working in public relations, ticket sales, and marketing. If your request simply said, "Dear Florida Marlins," the note might get thrown

1994
KANSAS CITY ROYALS
FAN INFORMATION

Jeff Montgomery
1993 American League
Rolaids Relief Man
Champion

Greg Gagne
1993 Royals
Player of the Year

Kevin Appier
1993 Royals
Pitcher of the Year

The 1994 Royals squeezed a lot into one 8 3/4-by 13 1/2-inch brochure, folded into fourths. On one side is the team's spring-training photo, along with a roster. On the reverse side is a history of the team's stadium, souvenir mail-order directions, a list of special giveaway events, and a cartoon of three players.

into a huge pile of similar mailings from fans. Instead, if you use the directory to find out the name of the public-relations director or other office staff member, your letter could zoom to the head of the class of fan requests.

Likewise, a letter that says, "Dear Sir: Please send me all your free stuff" isn't going to work. You're not as likely to get a special item if you don't ask for it. Writers of "send me everything" types of letters might receive a standard package with a schedule, sticker, and souvenir sales list. With a thoughtful, specific inquiry directed to a certain team worker, you might have better luck.

Even if you don't use a directory to find the roster of all team employees, read newspaper and magazine reports about your favorite clubs. Some articles might include clues in phrases such as "According to team spokesman Bill Ballclub . . . ." Copy down the name, and address your letter to that person.

Here's a sample postcard note:

Dear (insert name of team employee):

My family and I have been fans of the (insert name of team) for years. Even if we can't attend any games in person this year, we'll be following the team on radio and TV.

I'd be grateful if you could send us pocket schedules, a team roster, and sticker. Also, I'd like to know how to acquire a photo of (insert name) and other souvenirs. Please send a price list or catalog. Thank you.

Sincerely,

(insert your name)

(insert your address and ZIP code)

On-line access might also allow you (or your computer, at least) to contact a front-office employee. The Mariners and their pioneering on-line service provide a center for news of mail-order souvenirs and promotional items. Another center offers a list of all team employees and their job descriptions. The Mariners announced their electronic-mail (e-mail) address during a press conference, in hopes of serving the public. Instead of hearing only from fans in their region, the Mariners received correspondence from computer users worldwide.

Be creative, but be honest about what you want to receive. Would you like to write a report or give a speech in school about the team's history? If so, mention that in your letter. If you are interested in architecture, ask for details about the team's stadium. When a club has a new ballpark to brag about, such as Baltimore's Camden Yards, it creates new photos and brochures. Some fans make special trips and pay to tour popular stadiums, so teams make extra efforts to tout their home fields.

Nearly all teams have costumed mascots and are happy to send photos on request. Many teams also hire official artists. You might be able to spot the artists' names on some artwork or on an inside page of a program, and ask for information about them or for samples of their work. Any aspect of a current team is fair game for collectors. The more original you are in your request, the more likely it is that you'll get a detailed and original response.

In general, you should avoid three things when contacting teams by mail:

1. Don't lie. Some adults have asked for donations of autographs and equipment, promising that the items will be sold for charity. When the teams have discovered that the adults have actually kept or sold these items, they've reported the lawbreakers to authorities. If team employees get the idea you're trying to trick them, they could stop sending freebies to everyone.

2. Don't telephone. Sure, it's tempting to grab the telephone to save time. Don't waste your family's money on long-distance charges. Team employees are busy, struggling to talk with season-ticket holders, the media, and many others involved with the club on a daily basis. They spend any left-over time answering mail. Don't send faxes either—these also make extra work.

3. Don't complain if you don't get a response. No team has to send free merchandise and collectibles to fans, but thousands of collectors receive them each week. Although it may seem that teams must have money to spare, some major-league teams faced financial problems in the 1990s, and decided to save money by focusing only on fans in their own and nearby states.

CHOOSE YOUR MOMENT

Surprisingly, there is no bad time to write to a team. You have the best chances for a detailed reply at the start of the season, when the push for ticket sales is strong. If a team is in the middle of a losing season, your request for schedules and more could produce a better response than expected. The office employees may be hearing from fewer fans and ticket buyers, and may have more time to try harder to please remaining supporters.

Teams promote special events or seasonal anniversaries with giveaways and price breaks. This poster was designed to accompany an offer of discounted tickets made to churches, clubs, and other organizations.

Even in winter, teams may have new information. In December, spring-training schedules may be available. Teams will be eager to tell you more just after they've changed their logo or uniform. Also, if you write after the season has ended, you may discover discounted mail-order souvenirs.

Just after the World Series, write to your team to ask if a winter caravan or off-season fan festival is planned for your area. A winter caravan occurs when the ticket department takes its show on the road. Team members travel throughout surrounding states, giving speeches and signing autographs to drum up support for the upcoming season. A winter caravan might stop in communities hundreds of miles from a big-league town.

Fan festivals, on the other hand, are held only in the team's home city and can last three days. Imagine an amusement park designed around your favorite team. Question-and-answer sessions, autograph signings, screenings of films of season highlights, and the traditional hobby-dealer show are just a few of the activities that may be packed under one roof.

Unlike the winter-caravan pep rallies, there's always an admission charge at fan fests. But you'll likely get more than your money's worth because autographs and other freebies are given to all in attendance.

IF AT FIRST YOU DON'T SUCCEED... If you don't get responses from certain teams, simply concentrate on the clubs that will correspond with you. Even if the most responsive teams are not your personal favorites, you can acquire a trading stock to someday exchange for the memorabilia you really want.

There are teams of all levels, in all areas. Some last only a few years, such as the 1980s Florida-based Senior Baseball League, which consisted of teams of retired major leaguers in their 30s and 40s. In the 1990s unaffiliated minor-league teams began. These teams had no working agreements with big-league clubs. The Colorado Silver Bullets—a women's baseball team that played exhibition games against men because there were no other women's teams—was launched by Coors in 1994. If a team is of interest to you, gather memorabilia while you may.

Finally, don't forget college teams. Many collegiate coaches are former major leaguers, and today's college players can become next season's big-league rookies. Each college has a Sports Information Director, and many have large publicity staffs. These offices help sell tickets, work with the media, and please fans. They will be happy to respond to younger fans like you. You might grow up to play for their team, or become a season-ticket holder or a future corporate sponsor!

No matter what teams you choose to collect, remember that any team may have something for you. Keep in mind, too, that many clubs want fans to have items that promote their tickets, games, and players. While you're wondering what a team can do for you, the team is wondering the same thing about you. This partnership keeps collecting, and baseball, going strong.

Chapter Four

◆

Finding Finds

Everyone in baseball knows that kids don't stay kids forever. Kids become adults. Many become parents with kids of their own. If they start to love baseball when they are young, they'll maintain and share their commitment to the sport and its memorabilia when they're older. In other words, kids count.

Many players at stadiums will sign autographs for kids first, because they remember themselves as young fans. Front-office personnel and players alike often grew up as sports enthusiasts, asking their parents to take them to games, seeking players' autographs once they were there.

Although your youth can be an advantage when seeking collectibles, to have a better chance of getting autographs or memorabilia, make requests when you aren't in the middle of a crowd. For example, if a player agrees to give you a broken bat

This pin was available for free during a 1994 Dodgers game. The next week, the same pin could be bought for 76 cents with a gas purchase at Unocal stations. Some hobbyists wear the pins; others keep them in their original bags and on the original information cards.

minutes before the game starts, fifty other fans leaning over the rail may then demand the same treatment. Team members try to please as many people as they can, but may not be able to.

Thinking of the right people to ask, what to ask for, and when to ask requires more effort than simply plopping down some money for memorabilia. Young or beginning collectors may admire the unique, older, and more expensive memorabilia that are no longer available, and believe that their collections will never be as classy as those of rich, experienced hobbyists.

Not true. Even if some adult collectors spend thousands of dollars on an autograph or newspaper without blinking, odds are that they would rather have collected that same item when they

In 1982 you could get one of these color prints of Tommy Lasorda, or other Dodgers, only by making a fuel purchase at Union 76 stations in Southern California.

TOM LASORDA

were children. Quite likely, they're buying items that were popular and much less expensive during their childhoods. "When I was a kid, those were everywhere," might be an adult collector's typical comment.

Clubs in the majors seem less generous—or maybe less wasteful—these days. Major-league teams often recycle all types of equipment by shipping it to minor-league outlets for further use. Any additional equipment and supplies that a team doesn't ship to its own souvenir stores may be sold in huge groupings to memorabilia dealers.

The minor-league farm system, which develops new players, can be a gold mine for budget-minded collectors. Teams in the low minors (Rookie League and class A) may wear uniforms worn by All-Star big leaguers just one year ago. A fabric strip is sewn over the name of the major leaguer who wore the shirt before. Spot a minor leaguer on the field caught in the rain, and you just might see the previous, big-league occupant's name magically appear through the cloth.

Likewise, bats will pass through many hands. The Springfield (Illinois) Cardinals minor-league team garnered hobby fame by holding a "bat grab" day. Broken and extra bats stockpiled throughout the season were scattered onto the field during one of the last home games. Lucky children selected for the promotion were given limited time to run onto the field and grab a souvenir. Some bats had two numbers written on the knob, noting the jersey numbers of both the major and minor leaguers who took swings with the much-used piece of lumber.

RECYCLABLES

For years, the class-A team in Cedar Rapids, Iowa, sold broken bats for $1 apiece. Other teams in the minors have sold publications and memorabilia from past years available at lower prices than the ones from the current year. Sometimes, there are leftover premiums, but they're not displayed for sale. It never hurts to ask what else might be available, especially if the team has recently changed its name, logo, or uniform design.

WHAT'S IN A NAME?

During a single year in the early 1990s, more than a third of the minor-league teams in existence planned to change their names or their logos. Most retooled their names or the design of their team symbols simply to boost ticket and souvenir sales. Before this, such changes usually had occurred only when minors became part of a different major-league organization.

Following the 1994 season, the Pacific Coast League team in Tacoma, Washington, changed its name from the Tigers to the Rainiers (because of the nearby mountain, not because of the weather!). They had just switched affiliation from the Oakland Athletics to the Seattle Mariners, a big-league parent just one hour away. Not coincidentally, the minor-league owners chose the same name that had been held by a popular minor-league club in Seattle for more than 20 years before the Mariners arrived. The nostalgia evoked by the revival of the team name was a surefire way to guarantee a booming souvenir business. Longtime fans of the Tacoma team were sure to show their loyalty by wearing the current team's caps, jackets, and sweatshirts.

Tacoma Tigers

1987 BASEBALL SCHEDULE

⊗ *June 18*
Tigers vs. Oakland A's
⊗ *July 3*
Tacoma Athletic Commission
Fireworks Extravaganza

GAME INFO. 752-9161
RESERVATIONS 752-7707

TICKET PRICES

		Seniors, Children & Military
General Admission	2.75	Get 50¢ Discount On All
Reserved Seats	3.50	Daily Admission Tickets
Box Seats	4.00	

MEMBER OF THE PACIFIC COAST LEAGUE

Schedules document the history of a team. In 1995, for example, the Tacoma Tigers and its mascot became pieces of history when the team changed its name to the Rainiers and its major-league affiliation from the Oakland Athletics to the Seattle Mariners.

While non-collecting fans scramble to buy the brand-new merchandise of a transforming club in the minors, budget-saving hobbyists can swoop in to buy discounted souvenirs.

A souvenir can be anything you want it to be. One good example comes from Tacoma where, in the 1980s, the minor-league ballpark Cheney Stadium was remodeled. Old wooden seats were replaced with modern fiberglass models. The old seats were piled in a trash heap in front of the park, waiting to be hauled away. A few collectors picked through the piles and took home seats.

These treasure hunters got an added bonus: The seats weren't originally from Tacoma, but had been donated by the San Francisco Giants more than 25 years earlier. The seats came from Seals Stadium, a Pacific Coast League park that once hosted future Hall of Famers, such as Joe DiMaggio, and first-year San Francisco Giants, such as Willie Mays.

IN YOUR OWN BACKYARD

Not everyone gets to live near, or even visit, a professional baseball team every year. Some collectors don't even have pro ball in their states. Yet, the collectibles are there, quite likely in your hometown—if you know where to look.

Newspaper and magazine publishers and radio stations are found even in small towns. You may not hear or read about major- or minor-league baseball in your local publication, but the staff may be getting regular mailings from the teams. Your sports editor might be throwing away media guides, publicity photos, and other team collectibles every week.

This combination business card and postcard was offered as a free souvenir to collectors who dined at the Amana Colonies in Iowa. The owner of the restaurant had pitched in the majors throughout the 1940s.

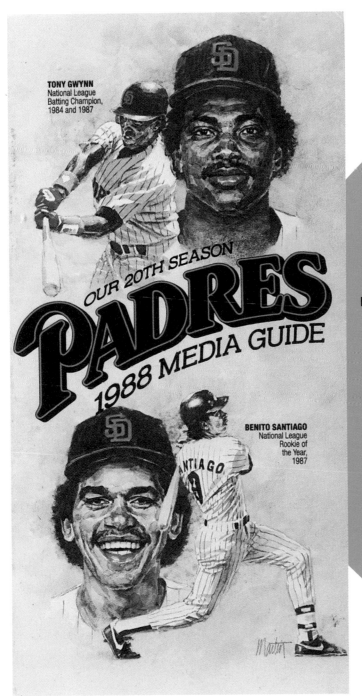

Despite their stunning cover artwork or photos—which often do not appear anywhere else—press guides aren't always sold to the public. Often, however, at season's end, reporters discard them. Watchful collectors might be able to add these 150-page media guides to their collections.

Reporters can attend games for free and sit in press boxes. Even if they don't report on the game, they'll get a special identification badge and a packet of press releases. These are sheets filled with statistics and information about all the players.

Newspapers receive laser photos, actual photographs sent over telephone lines by wire services like the Associated Press and transmitted like a fax. These photos provide a newspaper hundreds of miles from a ballpark with shots of a recent game. Because they are printed on thin paper, laser photos are thrown out or recycled. However, a few could wind up in your collection.

Write to the sports editors in your town. Explain what you collect and ask if they would save any mailings they receive for you. Offer to pick them up every week or two.

Add big-city newspapers to your list of places, too. If you are a Reds fan living in Arizona, you might be tempted to subscribe to Cincinnati newspapers to get daily news of your favorite team. Subscriptions may be too costly, though. Instead, write in advance to the circulation departments of the newspapers in your favorite team's city. Ask how to order the special edition that will carry the season preview about your team. Nowadays, newspapers will include posters, pullout magazine sections, and lots of other features in a special issue to honor the start of a new season. Also, if a team is hosting the All-Star game or makes the World Series, more special editions will be planned.

Some city newspapers have created other memorable tributes, too. In 1990 the Cincinnati

Enquirer sold T-shirts that pictured a full-color reprint of the newspaper page proclaiming the Reds' world championship over the Oakland A's. When the Twins reached the World Series in 1987, a Minnesota newspaper created a "Homer Hanky" for $1, and the proceeds went to charity. Fans attending games in Minneapolis waved the handkerchiefs to cheer the Twins.

For more information about acquiring out-of-state newspapers and magazines, ask your local librarian. The library also may be willing to give you old issues that will be discarded.

Your local bookstore is another possible treasure trove. Although you may not get anything free at bookstores, there are still numerous bargains. Look for markdowns. Baseball biographies are often on sale, and the sale price of the hardcover is often less than what the paperback sells for.

Used bookstores are also gold mines for collectors willing to dig. Often, used bookstores will sell titles for half or less of their original cover price. The trick is to figure out how the store employees group the used titles. The Nonfiction, Sports, or even Biographies sections could contain cheap collectibles.

Used-book sales held by public libraries can yield more finds, while putting your money to a worthy cause. After all, the library is the place where you can check out baseball titles beforehand, deciding which ones are good enough to add to your own collection. New books also are often sold at great savings by price clubs or special discount stores as a way to attract customers who might also buy larger, more expensive items.

Don't forget to ask your family and friends for ideas and help. Tell them what you want to add to your collection. They may be able to spot goodies for you at rummage sales or thrift stores. You might even be invited to help clean out a grandparent's attic or basement. Don't ever assume someone can't help you with your hobby. Your friends and family might surprise you years afterward with a late, but great, addition to your collection.

Chapter Five

◆

The Baseball (and Memorabilia!) Hall of Fame

Ever since the opening of the National Baseball Hall of Fame and Museum in 1939, the world has called Cooperstown, New York, "the birthplace of baseball." However, with more than 6,000 different items on display, Cooperstown could also be the site of a memorabilia collector's hall of fame.

No one may know more about the contents of Cooperstown's famed facility than registrar Peter Clark. By the 1990s he had spent more than a quarter of a century as a member of the museum staff, keeping track of all the objects in storage and on display.

"I keep records of all objects we have, entering a lot of that information on computer," Clark said. "I work on the business end of our collecting." That duty includes noting the history behind an object, the date it was given or loaned, the object's condition, and who donated it.

The Baseball Hall of Fame and Museum in Cooperstown, New York, houses more than 6,000 items of baseball memorabilia, including scrapbooks made by fans.

To maintain the historical value of the items in your collection, always be sure to record all the important information about the event and the object. Although this painter's cap, offered as a premium in a 1994 Dodgers Stadium promotion, may be rarer than most baseball cards from that same year, collectors may place little value on it. Why? There is no date on the cap linking it to a specific season.

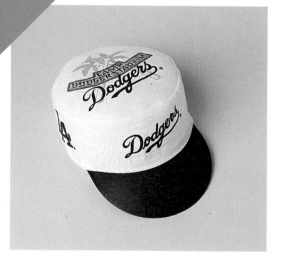

Of course, the museum pieces that get the most attention are often the bats, balls, or other equipment used in record-breaking moments, such as when Hank Aaron became baseball's all-time home-run king with 715 career round-trippers.

As collectors tour the Hall's museum, they concentrate on each memento displayed and wonder about its age, origin, or cash value on the collectibles market. Hobbyists ask, "How did the museum get that?" Surprisingly, some of Cooperstown's finest artifacts may once have been considered garbage.

For example, when you're in the ballparks exhibit of the museum, inspect the batting helmet rack and bricks salvaged from defunct Shibe Park in Philadelphia. Did Phillies team officials think to preserve these pieces of history before seeing their home field torn down in 1970? No. That took the imagination of photographer Bob Bartosz, who was nosing around the soon-to-be demolished site. For his own amusement, Bartoz saved a few tidbits from the upcoming scrap heap. Later that decade, as other old ballparks "bit the dust," he realized that the public would like seeing bits of the past.

"When the American League moved its office, we were called," said registrar Clark. "They wanted to clean out their files. So we hired a truck and went to New York City to pick up everything they didn't want." Clark and the staff's efforts saved correspondence and other historic papers from destruction. Now, the old A.L. papers sit in the Hall of Fame library archives, available to baseball writers and researchers.

THE SHAWON-O-METER

Clark laughed as he told of a memorable donation by two Chicago-area teenagers. "In the 1990s, two fellows, age seventeen to eighteen, contacted us," he remembered. "They had constructed what they called the Shawon-O-Meter." The sign, mounted on thick foam-core board and built in three large segments, showed the teens' support of Cubs shortstop Shawon Dunston. While attending Wrigley Field games, they'd hold up their sign whenever Dunston batted.

"The first side had space for his batting average, and these guys changed the numbers each time he batted," Clark says. "The back of the sign held the message, 'Vote for Shawon for the All-Star Game—The All-American Boy.'" Although the supportive sign didn't get Dunston elected as starting shortstop, his batting average climbed by more than 60 points throughout the season.

"We don't accept many fan-related items," Clark says. "But we thought this had historical merit. The owners of the sign had documented the item's use throughout the season." Radio and TV stations that had broadcast Cubs games had saluted the sign, as had newspaper articles. This attention, which the signmakers had noted, made the Shawon-O-Meter a part of the Cubs' 1990 history.

SORTING IT OUT

Signs, bricks, helmet racks—how does the staff decide which items will become part of the Hall's museum collection? "We have five staff members who try to meet each week and discuss potential donations," Clark said. The Hall's two major guidelines are that each item accepted must have historical significance, and that there should be no duplicate items in the museum's collection. The museum is a nonprofit organization and doesn't pay to collect any baseball artifact, no matter how historic. All Hall of Fame items are either received as gifts or are loaned to the museum to be displayed for limited amounts of time.

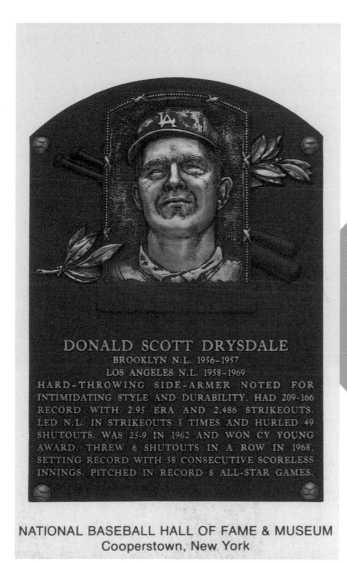

DONALD SCOTT DRYSDALE
BROOKLYN N.L. 1956-1957
LOS ANGELES N.L. 1958-1969
HARD-THROWING SIDE-ARMER NOTED FOR INTIMIDATING STYLE AND DURABILITY. HAD 209-166 RECORD WITH 2.95 ERA AND 2,486 STRIKEOUTS. LED N.L. IN STRIKEOUTS 3 TIMES AND HURLED 49 SHUTOUTS. WAS 25-9 IN 1962 AND WON CY YOUNG AWARD. THREW 6 SHUTOUTS IN A ROW IN 1968, SETTING RECORD WITH 58 CONSECUTIVE SCORELESS INNINGS. PITCHED IN RECORD 8 ALL-STAR GAMES.

NATIONAL BASEBALL HALL OF FAME & MUSEUM
Cooperstown, New York

Postcard-size reproductions of the member plaques are among the most popular of the Hall of Fame's souvenirs. Autograph collectors love them. In fact, the Hall of Fame provides them free to members who want to send them to players to autograph. The cards may also be puchased by mail or at the HOF gift shop.

"Our policy hasn't really changed since the beginning in 1939," Clark said. "We still have a policy of not buying memorabilia. We don't go to auctions, hobby shows, dealers, or card shops."

How can the Hall compete with the sellers of memorabilia? "Like any museum, we appeal to a person's higher instincts," Clark explained. "We still appeal to the sense of preserving history for future generations." To make the idea of giving a collectible to the Hall of Fame more attractive than the alternative of selling it elsewhere, all donors receive a certificate of appreciation from the Hall's board of directors, which is suitable for framing. Best of all, donors are given a pass that is good for a lifetime of free admission.

And, just like young collectors who can't seem to find a place to put it all, the Hall of Fame museum has space limitations. Frank Cirillo, designer for a "Baseball and the Movies" display, said he had to turn down an offering of the mechanical-bull billboard from the movie *Bull Durham,* which snorted smoke and flicked its tail whenever a player homered. "We couldn't accept it, because it was too big," Cirillo said. "If we had displayed it, we wouldn't have had space for anything else in the exhibit."

Turning down oversized memorabilia is nothing new for the museum. "The Cleveland Indians Booster Club offered us the Chief Wahoo mascot sign that stood outside Cleveland Stadium," Clark remembered, telling how the sign became a cast-off when the team moved to Jacobs Field in 1994. "We couldn't accept that, because it's more than two stories tall." While not all gifts made to the

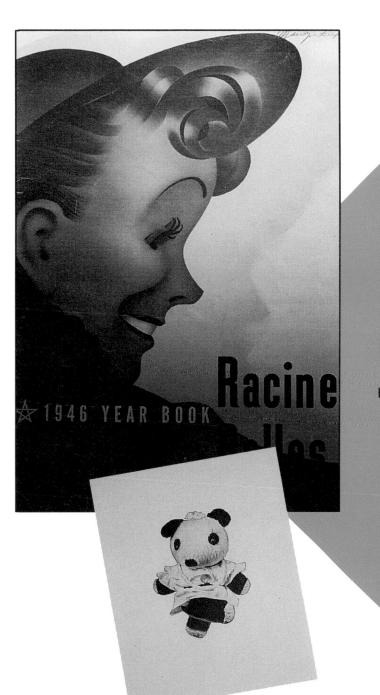

Remember the movie *A League of Their Own?* More than a half century ago, the real Racine Belles team produced a yearbook with a back-cover picture of their team mascot, a teddy bear wearing the Girls' League uniform.

Hall by teams, movie companies, or fans can be used, the offers are still valued by the staff.

The Hall of Fame is more than a museum. For people who love the game, it is also a paradise. It has a library and archives full of material from fans and collectors. In addition to books and magazines, this library collects photographs and rents them out to publishers of new books and magazines about baseball. One entire room of the library houses scrapbooks.

"Many of the scrapbooks were compiled by fans," Clark said.

Imagine. Even if you never played pro baseball, you and your scrapbook could make it into the Baseball Hall of Fame!

Chapter Six

◆

SABR, for Savers

*T*he Society for American Baseball Research, founded in 1971, is known by its acronym SABR (pronounced SAY-ber, just like the word "saber," meaning a pirate's sword).

In just two decades SABR had grown from its original 16 founders to nearly 7,000 members. This unique group is devoted to baseball memorabilia, not necessarily for their worth as collectibles but for their historical value.

Morris Eckhouse, the society's executive director in 1994, said that "less than one percent" of the membership was under age 18 at that time. But he added that "one of our founding members, Dan Ginsburg, was only 15 when he attended the first organizational meeting in Cooperstown in 1971." Today, Ginsburg is a successful author and lecturer on baseball history.

"We welcome any age," Eckhouse explained, "anyone who has an interest in baseball."

One of SABR's yearly publications is The National Pastime. Rare photos or unique pieces of artwork grace each cover. The work of this cover's artist, Bill Perry, has also appeared in The Sporting News.

THE
National ⚾ Pastime
A REVIEW OF BASEBALL HISTORY

Harvey Haddix

The Greatest Game Ever Pitched
(and the Braves had his signs)
—Steve Stout

Mark Alvarez: *The Cobb-Speaker Scandel* **Bob Tiemann:** *Of <u>course</u> there's clutch pitching*
Everardo Santamarina: *"He never hit against Castro"—The Hoak Hoax*
Ralph Moses: *The great Bid McPhee* **Gai Berlage:** *Women umps*
Howard Green: *A career in the minors*

SABR's focus on history gives members the opportunity to build their own baseball libraries quickly. *The National Pastime* and *Baseball Research Journal* are two annual softbound books created by members for members. Members research their favorite baseball subjects, then volunteer to write articles for both publications.

Members receive at least one SABR-created book each year. *The Negro Leagues Book*, a 382-page collective effort by the membership, was published in 1994. Cleveland Indians star Albert Belle was so moved by the depth of the book that he bought copies of the $25 book for the more than 100 surviving members of the Negro Leagues. The Negro Leagues Research Committee helped pay for printing by selling copies of the rare photos included in the book along with a poster of the painting of great Negro Leaguers featured on the cover.

The Negro League Research Committee sends out six newsletters yearly to members who focus on Negro Leagues history. One section in this newsletter, "Marketplace," reviews Negro Leagues-related commemorative merchandise, collectibles, and publications. It also notes prices and ways to obtain the best items.

Nationwide, members of Cleveland-based SABR have the chance to help out with more than a dozen different research committees. Besides the Negro Leagues, other subjects explored include collegiate baseball, ballparks, women in baseball, the minor leagues, umpires, nineteenth-century history, and baseball in Latin America. One of the newest SABR research committees is Pictorial, a group

PUBLICATIONS

A VALUABLE RESOURCE

dedicated to studying the history within the visual images of baseball photos—on cards, in newspapers, magazines, postcards.

SABR members of any age are likely to have saved books, photos, and other informative mementos from baseball's past over the years, along with SABR publications, which often feature writing by college students. *The Negro Leagues Book*, for example, contains 16 detailed college reports known as theses and dissertations. Many of the authors asked SABR members to find books, photos, and other materials to help them complete their work. Students may consider SABR their best-kept research secret. "We will serve students without discrimination to age," Eckhouse said.

When film historian Ken Burns made his epic 18-hour documentary about baseball history for public television, he relied on many SABR members to contribute photos for the nine episodes. SABR then helped the Public Broadcasting System (PBS) develop the "Learning Link," which provided a trivia contest for schools studying the *Baseball* series. Students had the chance to ask statistical questions of SABR members through computer linkups.

SABR members have been helping to collect the memories of former players, coaches, and other baseball employees, in much the same way that documentarian Burns did. Members of the Oral History Research Committee have volunteered to tape-record conversations with baseball's retirees. To preserve as much history as possible, the members interviewed men age 80 and older. The focus has been on baseball players of this age because they played in an era when fewer facts were

Avid memorabilia collectors know that baseball-related publications can be found anywhere. This is a newsletter from a group that provides weekly pregame church services for players during major- and minor-league seasons.

BASEBALL CHAPEL

NEWS

21st
SEASON

SUMMER
1993

All-Star Chapel Speaker:
DAVE DRAVECKY

Dave Dravecky has captured the hearts of Baseball fans as well as those who have heard his story. Born in 1952 in Boardman, Ohio, he graduated from Youngstown State University, was married and drafted by the Pittsburgh Pirates all in 1978. After a few years in the Minors he was brought up to the Majors in 1982 with the Padres. After five years with the Padres where he pitched in the National League Championship Series and the World Series he was traded to the Giants and also pitched in the National League Championship Series in 1987.

Opening day 1988 he shut out the Dodgers but later that season a tumor was discovered and in October half the deltoid muscle in his pitching arm was removed. In 1989 rehabilitation started and in August he pitched a 4-3 win over Cincinnati, more than a year since he last pitched.

We'll all remember the next start in Montreal. During the game the arm snapped and the arm was broken again during the celebration of the Giants going to the World Series.

But in November the cancer returned and Dave retired from Baseball. The next summer the arm, shoulder, shoulder blade and left side of the collarbone were amputated.

Jan and Dave have gone through a lot of pain, loss of family, suicide of a friend, and deep depression. Dave will be speaking on some of his experiences which are in his new book, <u>When You Can't Comeback.</u>

Through their suffering Jan and Dave have been an encouragement to thousands. We're very happy the Baseball family will have a chance to hear him at the All-Star Game Chapel Service.

Favorite Verses: Tom Foley, Pirates - "That if you confess with your mouth, 'Jesus is Lord'", and believe in your heart that God raised Him from the dead, you will be saved, for it is with your heart that you believe and are justified, and it is with your mouth that you confess and are saved." Romans 10:9,10

preserved, and they may not live as long as last year's retirees will. All the tape recordings are donated to the Baseball Hall of Fame's library, so they can be borrowed and studied by writers, students, fans, and historians.

Eckhouse was convinced that young people working with the oral historians could make surprising contributions. "They might do better than our older members," he said. "Young people might be more open-minded about baseball, asking questions from new perspectives." Any member of SABR can volunteer for the oral-history research committee. In the past, the committee chairperson has asked members to interview former baseball employees (anyone who made a living from the sport, not just players) who live nearby.

A VALUABLE LINK

The organization newsletter, *SABR Bulletin*, is published 10 times yearly. Each issue contains "Research Exchange," a list of members who seek information on certain baseball topics. The research is always shared again and again. Knowledge is not fun if it's hoarded.

This may be why some SABR history hunters might frown if you confuse them with traditional hobbyists. "Some members may bristle at the word 'collector,'" Eckhouse admitted. "They may collect cards, but they may also dislike the idea that collectors are concerned only about prices, and won't use their collections for research purposes."

Yet SABR members include some collectors who want to understand the history behind their memorabilia, who appreciate the links provided by the newsletter and the membership address directory.

Knowing where to find others who share your specific baseball interests is useful to fans of any age. More than 30 regional SABR groups exist across America. Additional members are found in many other countries, including Canada, Mexico, and Great Britain. "SABR is a vehicle for kids everywhere, especially those in areas removed from pro ball," Eckhouse explained.

Some SABR members have personal motives for joining the group. "Some may have a relative who played pro baseball and join to learn more about the family member's career," Eckhouse said. "Or someone from their neighborhood may have been in baseball."

Eckhouse explained that, when he was young, his interest in baseball grew as a result of his saving, studying, and reading cards, magazines, yearbooks, and other memorabilia. "SABR is for anyone interested in reading, learning, and talking about baseball," he said. "We'd welcome kids. We were all kids once."

Chapter Seven

◆

More About Memorabilia

Although most books and magazines about the hobby of collecting baseball memorabilia focus on cards, or the thousands of dollars spent on uniforms and other ultra-rare memorabilia, new resources are springing up yearly for dedicated hobbyists of all levels, ages, and incomes. Check out this sampling of resources to get started.

Baseball American Directory (P.O. Box 2089, Durham, NC 27702. Telephone: 800-845-2726). Although team addresses can be found for free in library almanacs or telephone books, this directory gives an advantage to anyone wanting to contact a team's publicity department directly. Be sure to use the newest directory to contact team representatives, because teams change their employees frequently and clubs change addresses more often than you'd think. If you can't purchase the current year's directory at a bookstore, order it from the publisher.

Baseball Hall of Fame and Museum (Box 590, Cooperstown, NY 13326). The HOF will forward autograph-request mail to all members. Likewise, the Hall has a mail-order catalog of memorabilia and souvenirs, which is free upon request. Among the best bargains offered by the museum are postcards picturing the induction plaques of each Hall of Fame member. These can be ordered in sets or individually. The second option is the best, because you can update your collection every time the Hall adds a few new members without buying another set of 200-plus postcards.

Encyclopedia of Sports Memorabilia and Price Guide (9171 Wilshire Blvd., Suite 300, Beverly Hills, CA 90210). This magazine, from the publishers of *Trading Cards* magazine, is published six times yearly. *Encyclopedia* differs from *SCD* in that it offers some color photos and more pricing information on older memorabilia. Still, it's one of the few "other than cards" publications in the hobby. Also, beginning collectors can benefit from the "how-to" articles, which offer, for example, tips for shopping at flea markets and the specifics of collecting sports newspapers.

Negro Leagues Baseball Museum (Lincoln Building, 1601 East 18th St., Kansas City, MO 64108-1646). This museum publishes a newsletter and sells souvenirs by mail.

Ray Medeiros (P.O. Box 60249, Colorado Springs, CO 80960-0249) and *Vic Pallos* (658 Arden Ave., Glendale, CA 91202). Both of these men are avid

Anything can become a collectible someday. Free ballots like these have been issued since the early 1970s, allowing fans to vote for players to start the All-Star Game. Most were returned or thrown away, but would be a great document to have in your collection.

collectors who have produced their own stadium postcards, using many rare ballpark photos from their own collections. Their postcards with their vintage photographs are much less expensive than actual postcards from bygone years would be. Write to either one of them for prices and other specifics.

Right on Schedules (c/o Keith Gadbury, 204 North Charro Ave., Thousand Oaks, CA 91320). This newsletter lists many types of new skeds (from all sports) discovered each month. *ROS*, which offers low-cost classified ads, is a good way to find traders by mail.

Society for American Baseball Research (SABR) (P.O. Box 93183, Cleveland, OH 44101). Yearly dues are inexpensive considering all the free newsletters and publications that members get by mail. If you like to read and learn about baseball, and would like to help preserve the history of the sport, think about joining SABR.

The Sports Americana Baseball Address List (Edgewater Book Company, P.O. Box 40238, Cleveland, OH 44140). This address directory is updated every two years. An old issue may have old addresses, and you'll waste stamps trying to track players down. Again, if your bookstore doesn't have this book, contact the publisher.

Sports Collectors Digest (700 East State St., Iola, WI 54990). Published weekly and intended for advanced collectors, *SCD* offers more non-card coverage than any other hobby publication.

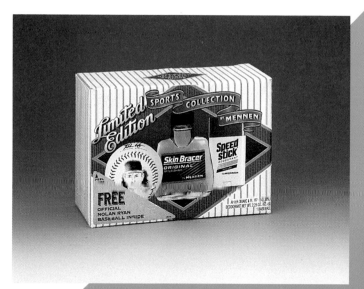

Collectors who paid less than $10 in 1994 for this gift set got not only a box with stats and photos of Nolan Ryan, but also a baseball with a portrait of Ryan by popular sports artist Christopher Paluso. Just because the ball is labeled "limited edition," there's no way of knowing how many were—or will be—made. Collect items that you enjoy, regardless of their potential value.

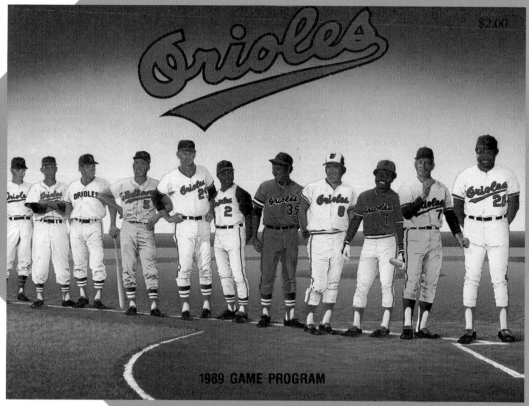

1989 GAME PROGRAM

The 1989 Orioles program magazine featured a fantasy painting showing players from different eras modeling the various uniforms the team had worn over the previous 35 years. For $5, fans could order a poster of the cover image.

Surprisingly, the magazine's advertisements of memorabilia are sometimes more helpful than the articles. You may find advertisements for self-published books about a particular hobby specialty. The books may be no more than photocopied typed pages stapled together, but the information may be invaluable—some of these authors checklist their mammoth collections while sharing with readers all they've learned through years in the hobby.

In each issue, classified ads note collectors who want to trade ticket stubs, schedules, stadium postcards, or other memorabilia from their regions. You may discover a collector with the same interests as yours who will trade by mail or who lives in your community!

Standard Catalog of Baseball Cards (Krause Publications, 700 East State St., Iola, WI 54990). This company, which brings you *SCD*, updates its massive softcover encyclopedia every two years. Despite its card-related title, this publication is a good source for checklists of postcards, photos, pins, and other cardlike collectible sets issued by teams, food companies, or other sources. Tidbits about how the collectibles were issued initially make the book educational and fun.

If you've mastered the mail as a hobby resource and have a computer, scout the bulletin boards and chat groups of various on-line services for other baseball-memorabilia collectors. Card companies and memorabilia manufacturers were among the last corporate giants to consider communicating with customers by computer.

Getting autographs by e-mail has been an impossibility because of the limited time and training of celebrities. Team employees, however, have made slow but steady progress in becoming on-liners. For World Wide Web users, the e-mail address of the Seattle Mariners, baseball's on-line pioneers, is: http://www.mariners.org/.

Remember, the best way to stay informed about the hobby is to communicate with other collectors, in person, by mail, or by computer. If you have good luck, or no luck, in searching for memorabilia, talk to others about it. When others can learn from your victories and defeats and you can learn from theirs, everyone wins.

Glossary

*Y*ears ago, vendors at ballparks would shout, "Get your scorecards. You can't tell the players apart without a scorecard!" Back then, jerseys only displayed numbers, not player names, and numerical rosters were included in the scorecards so you would know who's who.

Consider this your hobby scorecard, so you can "know the lingo"—learn the hobby language.

advertisement—usually, a full-page of a magazine, featuring one or more players endorsing a product. Some collectors would value the page of an old magazine if it contained an ad of Stan Musial selling cereal.

airbrushed—describes cards that have had their team logos removed from photos, because the cards are not licensed and approved by Major League Baseball.

all-star ballot—the official form used by fans to vote for players in the All-Star Game.

assorted—the term used by hobby dealers for "grab bags," or quantities of items they repackage for resale, to indicate that duplicates, or more than one of the same item, may be contained in the grouping. Assorted does not mean that all the items are different.

authentication—any proof that the description of the collectible is true. Usually a written statement by the player who owned the equipment, the fan who obtained the autograph in person, or anyone (from the team or elsewhere) who knows that the item is authentic.

ballpark—a baseball stadium.

box-bottoms—boxes that held foil or wax packs of baseball cards and may have cards printed on their sides or bottoms.

coin—a metal or plastic disc that pictures a player or team logo to commemorate an event or record.

collectible—1. anything worth saving. 2. something other than cards, such as autographs, photos, publications, etc.

collector issue—a collectible that is designed mostly for the collector market and sold first only by hobby dealers, without being used to promote or sell other goods or services.

commemorative—1. any collectible made to salute a certain event. These items are dated and may be sold only during the following season, or for a shorter period. 2. an authorized reprint of cards or memorabilia, sometimes issued again to denote an anniversary of some event, sometimes having special markings to indicate the second release.

common—1. easy to get, available often or everywhere. 2. a player with little or no stardom who commands little attention from collectors or financial value from dealers.

defunct—similar to "extinct," a term for baseball stadiums and teams that no longer exist. Defunct stadiums include Ebbets Field in Brooklyn and the Polo Grounds in New York. Defunct teams are teams that have moved to new cities, such as the Brooklyn Dodgers who moved to Los Angeles and the New York Giants who moved to San Francisco. Some teams change their whole name, as when the Washington Senators moved in 1961 and became the Minnesota Twins.

double—an extra, or duplicate, of an item in your collection.

dust jacket—the outer covering of a hardcover book, containing pictures and other information.

facsimile—an autograph that looks like the original signature but has been mass-produced on baseballs, photos, or other souvenirs.

first edition—the initial printing of a publication. Often, a first edition may be printed in a smaller quantity than later print runs, and so that edition is rarer. Subsequent printings for books, yearbooks, and programs may include new photos or other changes.

full ticket—the complete unused ticket from a baseball game.

game-used—describes equipment worn or used by players during games.

giveaways—souvenirs or promotional items given only to fans attending a certain game. Used to increase attendance.

Hartlands—a Wisconsin plastics company that produced sports-related toy statues in the late 1950s and early 1960s. A generic Little League player and 18 actual major leaguers were included in the baseball series. The statues were reissued in 1989.

index card—measuring 3 by 5 inches, also known as a "recipe card," and used for autographs.

laser photo—a photo of a game and/or players, sent to newspapers by a news agency, such as the Associated Press, by way of a laser printer. Printed on thin photographic paper.

logo—a symbol or insignia displayed on a team's uniforms, caps, and jackets.

lot—a grouping of related collectibles, resold by a hobby dealer.

medallion—see *coin*.

media guide—a pocket-size mini-encyclopedia issued by a team and containing tons of statistics. Although media guides were once available only to reporters and sports announcers, many clubs now sell them to fans.

memorabilia—1. items that stir memories of a certain time or event. 2. collectibles other than cards.

official baseball—a baseball, not necessarily game-used, that carries the authorized marking of its exact major or minor league. For example, the San Francisco Giants use National League baseballs.

premium—1. a prize, considered to be a collectible, given when someone buys a particular product or service, such as cereal or an oil change. 2. a free item given to fans who attend a certain game.

press guide—see *media guide*.

program—a team-produced magazine sold at games. Many programs include scorecards.

proof of purchase—a boxtop, UPC (universal price code), package section, or cash-register receipt used to qualify the purchaser of a product or service for a mail-in offer. Companies boost sales of their products by offering cards and memorabilia to anyone who makes a specified purchase.

regional—a collectible issued in only one city or area of the country, usually in the area nearest to the team represented.

reissue—additional, authorized distribution of cards or memorabilia, sometimes conducted years after the first issue. Often, the same item will be reissued with only minor changes, to indicate the commemorative nature of the release.

replica—1. equipment that duplicates actual game-used items but is mass-produced and sold through hobby dealers or sporting-goods stores. 2. an authorized copy of a collectible.

revised—describes a later edition of a book, poster, or any collectible, usually made to add information to or correct a mistake in the previous edition.

schedule—a listing of a team's games for a season, also called a *sked*. Most schedules are pocket-size, often with a player's photo on the front. Schedules can also be printed on posters, cups, pop cans, or other surfaces.

scorecard—often only two pages, with spaces to detail the progress of each inning of a game. Some clubs include these with programs; others sell them separately.

scored—describes a program or scorecard written on by a fan who kept inning-by-inning notes of the game's progress.

scrapbook—a homemade collection of photos, newspaper clippings, and related items pasted or affixed onto blank pages and held in a notebook or similar binder.

sked—see *schedule*.

skedder or skedhead—a nickname for someone who collects schedules.

souvenir—1. a hotly debated term. Considered by some to be uncollectible merchandise, such as hats or T-shirts, produced in unlimited quantities for years, without any noted changes. 2. any item that holds personal meaning.

sponsor—a company that helps provide premiums or giveaway items and advertises on those collectibles.

sports information office—a college department, headed by a sports information director (SID), that works with the media to publicize teams.

Donruss and other companies formerly sold cards in waxy wrappers, like this one from 1985, creating the hobby term "wax pack." Most cards produced in the 1980s remained in collectors' hands, but most of the wrappers did not.

stadium postcards—postcards picturing baseball stadiums.

Starting Lineups—action figures depicting baseball players, made by Kenner Toys since 1988. New editions are issued yearly, often with cards, posters, medallions, or other premiums.

stationery—a team's official paper and envelope displaying the team's address and logo.

stock—the quality and thickness of paper or cardboard of a card, photo, or other collectible.

stub—the half of a baseball ticket that is detached and returned as the fan enters the stadium.

team issue—memorabilia created and sold, or given away, by a pro team.

team postcards—postcard-size photos, many without postcard backs, picturing each member of a team. Some sets are sold by teams; others are available only by writing to the individual players.

unlicensed—describes memorabilia that do not have the approval of Major League Baseball and/or the Players Association. Unlicensed photos are sometimes airbrushed to remove identifying team logos.

unopened—describes a collectible that has never been removed from its original wrapping or a package that has never been opened.

UPC—universal price code. The set of bars scanned by a computer that indicate an item's price. The UPC may be required as proof of purchase by companies offering collectibles to customers by mail.

variation—a different version of the same item. For instance, a team photo of a player might be issued with facsimile authographs and, as a variation, without them.

wrapper—the original package containing baseball cards. Throughout the 1980s, most baseball wrappers were made of wax paper.

yearbook—a team-produced publication, previewing the team's upcoming year. Player photos make up most of a yearbook, but biographies and articles may be included, too.

Index